RESTORING THE "UNWRITTEN ALLIANCE" IN BRAZIL–UNITED STATES RELATIONS

In response to Brazil's recent emergence as a global economic and political player, the United States must reformulate its diplomatic and security strategy with the world's 7th largest economy and Latin America's biggest military. Genuine concerns with sovereignty and reciprocity, along with negative American stereotypes that permeate Latin American culture, will complicate this task. Nevertheless, there is opportunity to bring the U.S.—Brazil diplomatic and security relationships closer together to build strategic partnership based on common interests throughout the world.

This paper proposes ways to strengthen these relationships through feasible actions that will yield immediate and long-lasting benefits. If U.S. leaders fail to respond to this diplomatic challenge, Brazil's leaders may reluctantly seek more advantageous diplomatic, security, and economic relationships elsewhere to the detriment of important U.S. interests in the Western Hemisphere.

Introduction

The primary challenge the United States faces in the 21st Century according to historian and diplomat Joseph Nye "is not one of decline but what to do in light of the realization that even the largest country cannot achieve the outcomes it wants without the help of others."[1] Acknowledging Brazil as a genuine partner is problematic for the U.S. leaders since the United States historically has exercised tremendous unilateral influence in South American affairs throughout the 19th and 20th Centuries. Today, U.S. hubris lingers in the nation's relations with Brazil. This residual attitude prompts some U.S. leaders to consider any Brazilian disregard for U.S. interest as an affront. Instead of regarding Brazil's economic growth as a challenge to U.S. hegemony, U.S. leaders should commend it as a regional achievement. Additionally, some current perceptions of the two countries' strategic interests continuing to diverge are historically shortsighted. It affirms a U.S. failure to adapt long-range diplomatic strategies to match the global rise of many nations throughout the world. Undeniably, the United States needs Brazil--now and in the future.

<u>A Global Power</u>

Economically, Brazil is becoming the most important country to the United States in the Western Hemisphere. Brazil will become the fifth largest world economy by 2015, while Canada will be eleventh and Mexico fifteenth.[2] "By the end of 2009, Brazil's economy represented forty percent of the total Gross Domestic Product (GDP) of Latin America and the Caribbean, and fifty-five percent of the GDP of South America alone."[3] Brazil will host both the 2014 World Cup and the 2016 Olympics; accordingly, it is investing billions of dollars in infrastructure and security improvements throughout the country. Additionally, a new oil field has been discovered off the coast of Rio de Janeiro. This discovery has drawn great interest from the United States, which is seeking oil autonomy from the Middle East. This offshore oil field and others will double Brazil's output of petroleum by 2020.[4]

Recently, Secretary of State Clinton proclaimed a "new 21st Century reality—that GDP matters more than military might."[5] Her pronouncement reprioritized economics to the forefront of U.S. foreign policy. She cited Brazil and India as examples of 21st Century economic success.[6] As U.S. foreign policy focuses more on economics, the U.S. relationship with Brazil assumes greater importance. If economics have become the primary interest in U.S. foreign policy, then failure to build a stronger strategic partnership with Brazil will be a huge opportunity lost for substantial economic trade and growth. Already Brazil has concluded Common Market of the South (MERCOSUR) free trade agreements with Israel, along with a separate trade arrangement with Egypt.[7] Additionally, Brazil has entered into special trading agreements with South Africa and India, which are also rapidly growing global economies.[8] The European Union and various other countries have recognized Brazil's rise and future economic potential. They too plan to make the most of what Brazil's economy has to offer.

Tides of History

The United States has not viewed its bilateral relationship with Brazil through the lens of history. Brazil's recent economic growth should not be regarded as a miracle of a third world country. Rather, Brazil's rise represents the re-emergence of a global economic and diplomatic player from the early to mid-20th Century. At that time, the United States supported Brazil's preeminence in South America. President Teddy Roosevelt even hoped that Brazil would be the responsible party for supporting the Monroe Doctrine within the region.[9] Approximately twenty years later, Brazil became one of the original members of the League of Nations, and committed the only Latin American ground forces to the Allied cause during World War II, deploying an entire division to Europe. Unfortunately, Brazil's rise to preeminence in South America was interrupted by authoritarian military rule that sapped its international credibility for 21 years. Only now has Brazil regained its capability and potential for regional and global leadership. And, like before, there is a window of opportunity for the United States to redefine the U.S.—Brazil strategic relationship and restore the "Unwritten Alliance"[10] that was initially established by Secretary of State Elihu Root, whose work towards greater Pan-American understanding contributed to his receiving the Nobel Peace Prize in 1912.

<u>Consistent Player</u>

Today, Brazil sees itself as a regional leader.[11] Its strategy is not to disrupt or disturb any multi-lateral organizations, despite its growing power, "but to adapt them and employ [its strengths] as platforms to advance Brazilian interests."[12] This strategy nests nicely with two of President Rousseff's areas for action: "diversifying relations by forging stronger economic and political ties with other nations of the developing world; and supporting multilateralism by pushing for the democratization of global governance."[13] Brazil has recently proven its unfaltering pursuit of these goals, and this commitment has not been lost on the other 11 South American countries. In view of Brazil's significant economic progress, its neighbors acknowledge that Brazil is now a serious global player and economic powerhouse. Proximity to Brazil will benefit these South American countries; and position regional relations to eliminate the need to look elsewhere for economic support.

Historically, Brazil has already exercised leadership in conflict disputes between other countries in the region. In 1942, it played a key role in resolving the Ecuador—Peru War. Brazil arbitrated a peace settlement between them once again in 1995.[14] Likewise, Brazil has shared hydroelectric power with its neighbors; it has entered into cooperative security agreements, brokered distribution of fresh water, and managed regional environmental programs. However, Brazil's government has had difficulty with indigenous minority groups. For example, it is constantly challenged to persuade the Amazon aboriginals the benefits of certain regional infrastructure projects.

Still, through protracted negotiations, it has generally compensated displaced and dispossessed peoples.[15] Essentially, Brazil is growing into its role as the regional leader.

The United States once held this difficult position in South America exercising leadership through the Monroe Doctrine and Rio Treaty—and receiving much dissent along the way. Now it is Brazil that is criticized for both taking action and not taking enough action. But, Brazil has the wherewithal to successfully manage this transition. History is on its side: Brazil has remained at peace with its neighbors for nearly 150 years. No other emerging power in the world enjoys this kind of accomplishment.

Brazil's Defense Minister Celso Amorim has recently stated that his government's goal is to transform South America into a true "Peace Zone."[16] Brazil has largely accomplished this goal.[17] The United States should actively support Brazil's goal of a continental "Peace Zone." Such U.S. support will help convince the majority of Brazilians and Latin Americans that the primary U.S. interest is not to pursue imperial power and resource domination, but to promote international trade, investment, and security. Indeed, greater leadership roles for responsible countries in the global system actually strengthen U.S. worldwide interests and U.S. domestic security.[18]

Understanding Motivation

The United States, however, must also do a better job understanding how Brazil approaches diplomacy and difficult problems. In terms of interest versus values, Brazil emphasizes it constitutional values more than at any other time in its history. Self-determination, non-intervention, defense of peace, peaceful settlement of conflicts, repudiation of terrorism and racism, cooperation among peoples for the progress of mankind, and granting of political asylum are among the salient constitutional values

5

that Brazil uses to shape its international relations today.[19] Out of these, the peaceful settlement of disputes is highlighted in the preamble of its constitution. Indeed, it is the singular driving force behind Brazil's foreign policy.[20]

For example, Brazil has been exhibiting its constitutional values of non-intervention and peaceful settlement of conflicts when dealing with truculent Iran. At times, implementation of Brazil's brand of diplomacy upsets U.S. leaders. However, Brazil's official position has generally been historically consistent with its values and past actions. The United States seems to have been ignorant of Brazilian core values when it comes to diplomacy. U.S. failure to acknowledge Brazil's values oriented diplomacy has contributed to deteriorated relations in the past and enduring negative stereotypes.

As a non-permanent member of the UN Security Council (UNSC) in 2010, Brazil voted against implementing sanctions on Iran. In its minority vote with Turkey, Brazil claimed that "sanctions will most probably lead to the suffering of the people of Iran and will play in the hands of those, on all sides, that do not want dialogue to prevail. Past experiences in the U.N., notably the case of Iraq, show that the spiral of sanctions, threats and isolation can result in tragic consequences."[21] In this case, Brazil acted according to its core principle of the peaceful settlement of disputes. In addition, Brazil, along with Turkey, did not believe they were allowed enough time to culminate their tentative agreement with Iran.[22] Brasília's principal complaint was the perceived rush to sanctions. Likewise, Brazil's abstention the following year on UNSCR 1973, which authorized U.N. member states to take all necessary measures to protect civilians under threat of attack in Libya, also demonstrated Brazil's consistent pursuit of peaceful diplomacy. Explaining Brazil's abstention, Ambassador Maria Luiza Ribeiro Viotti argued that "No military action alone would succeed in ending the conflict. Protecting civilians, ensuring lasting settlement and addressing the legitimate demands of Libyan citizens demanded a political process."[23] The ambassador was somewhat prophetic: former rebel and pro-Qaddafy militias are still fighting months after the death of Momar Qaddafy. Civil War could likely break out, since no governments have been willing to provide a stabilization force after the overthrow, thereby creating a huge security vacuum.[24] Again, Brazil's vote affirmed their value of non-intervention and peaceful settlement of conflicts. This common thread of values is woven throughout Brazilian diplomacy. Along with 137 other countries, Brazil recently supported a U.N. General Assembly vote condemning Syrian leaders' on-going violations on their citizens' human rights. Also Brazil supported an Arab League plan for a political transition in Syria.[25] Brazil's support, which moved from an earlier abstention last December on a similar resolution, still focuses on a peaceful political transition, not a violent one.[26] Whether it is resolving a border conflict in South America, dealing with the erratic Hugo Chavez in Venezuela, or negotiating with the radical Islamic regime in Iran, Brazil has shown itself consistent in word and deed to its core constitutional values. Brazil is a responsible and rational actor in its foreign policy and regional relations.

Diplomatic Recommendations

Several proposals would set the U.S.-Brazil relationship in a positive path for the next twenty years. They would also allay Brazil's historic concerns for sovereignty and reciprocity. First, the United States needs to support Brazil's effort to gain a permanent seat on the United Nations Security Council (UNSC). Second, the President needs to update the National Security Strategy (NSS) to more accurately acknowledge Brazil's emerging global status. Third, the United States needs to take practical measures to support Brazil's leadership in South America and its role in multilateral regional organizations. Implementation of these recommendations will garner immediate reciprocal benefits from the Brazilian government, and lay the groundwork for future bilateral cooperation both regionally and globally. Stronger U.S.–Brazil relations will bolster homeland, regional, and international security.

The United States needs to formally endorse Brazil's bid for a permanent seat on the United Nation's Security Council (UNSC). The United States has extended this support to India, but not Brazil. Brazil's nominal gross domestic product (GDP) is projected to grow to the fifth largest in the world by 2015, while India's will grow only to ninth largest, immediately behind Russia.[27] India's GDP may surpass Brazil's in the future based on the purchasing power parity (PPP) methodology. However, once PPP GDP is adjusted per capita, Brazil will remain ahead of India in 2015.[28] Further, "Unlike India, [Brazil] has no insurgents, no ethnic and religious conflicts nor hostile neighbors."[29] It is problematic that India should receive a permanent UNSC seat before Brazil before resolving its conflict in Kashmir and Jammu with Pakistan.[30] In sharp contrast, Brazil is not encumbered by any such state conflicts. Any future U.N. political agreement regarding Kashmir will be severely limited by an Indian veto on the UNSC if this proposed agreement is not in New Delhi's best interest. Other permanent members of the UNSC–France, United Kingdom, and Russia--all affirmed their support for Brazil's bid for a permanent UNSC seat.[31] However, China remains uncommitted to both Brazil and India. Vociferous against Japan's candidacy for a permanent UNSC seat, China

8

has remained silent with regards to India. It is unlikely that China will support India's bid for a permanent UNSC seat due to its growing strategic partnership with the United States to counter China's military rise. Also, China does not want to jeopardize its growing friendship with Pakistan. If China does eventually support Brazil's bid to the Security Council, then the United States will remain the last hold-out. Last March President Obama endorsed the concept of an equal partnership.[32] But to be equal partners, both Brazil and the United States should be seated side-by-side on the UNSC as permanent members. Failure to endorse Brazil's bid to occupy a permanent seat on the UNSC will confirm Brazil's lingering suspicions that "the United States commitment to a mature relationship between equals is largely rhetorical."[33]

At the earliest opportunity, the President, should advance Brazil's position in the U.S. National Security Strategy from secondary interest to one of primary interest. Informed by this higher priority, Brazil's leaders will be assured on U.S. intentions to improve bilateral relations and cooperation across a wide range of security and economic issues throughout the world, particularly in South America. This re-prioritization will also lend legitimacy to President's Obama's pledge to treat Brazil as an equal partner, not a junior one. The NSS declares: "We are working to build deeper and more effective partnerships with other key centers of influence—including China, India, and Russia, as well as increasingly influential nations such as Brazil, South Africa, and Indonesia."[34] This syntax clearly delineates two groupings of nations. First, it lists China, India, and Russia as key centers of influence. Next, it lists Brazil, South Africa, and Indonesia as increasingly influential nations. Both China and Russia already occupy permanent seats on the UNSC affirming that they are key centers of influence.

Listing Brazil in the NSS as only an "increasingly influential nation" after considering the evidence of its economic power is unsound. Regardless, designating India a "key center of influence" is consistent with U.S. support for India's bid for a permanent seat on the UNSC. Further, the United States and India are already strategic partners because of shared concerns over a potentially hostile China. However, there are enormous differences in security, diplomatic, economic, and democratic contributions to international order between South Africa and Indonesia, on one hand, and Brazil, on the other hand. The strategic signation of Brazil as an increasingly influential nation and not a "key center of influence" supports former U.S. Ambassador Luigi Einaudi's view that "Washington's identification of Brazil with Latin America and the Third World hampers its appreciation of Brazil's importance to the United States."[35] Consider this: South Africa's and Indonesia's economies are respectively the 28th and 18th in the world. Significantly larger, Brazil hosts the world's 7th largest economy in the world.[36] Acknowledging Brazil's global status in the NSS would foster a stronger relationship. It would place Brazil on equal ground with other major global players such as China and Russia. And it would require Congress, the State Department, and the Department of Defense to give greater attention to our new equal partner to the south.

Interestingly, the 2011 U.S. National Military Strategy (NMS) actually supports South American regional structures and implies Brazil's leadership: "We welcome efforts by Brazil and our other regional partners to establish economic and security mechanisms, such as the South American Defense Council (SADC)." The SADC is a sub-organization of the Union of South American Nations (UNASUR).[37] It was modeled after the European Union, whose long-term goals of continental integration are similar.

Another regional South American organization not mentioned in the NMS is MERCOSUR, in which Brazil has become the natural leader due to its expansive economy. Through these organizations, Brazil has exercised regional leadership by addressing regional problems "without having to turn to extra-regional powers, such as the United States."[38] In the NSS, President Obama specifically cited Brazil's exceptional role in Latin America: "We welcome Brazil's leadership and seek to move beyond dated North-South divisions to pursue progress on bilateral, hemispheric, and global issues."[39] These policy statements clearly indicate that the United States prefers to work with any organization, sovereign or multi-lateral, that is proactively working to solve problems. UNASUR, MERCOSUR, and even the Community of Latin American and Caribbean States (CELAC), are U.S. potential partners for hemispheric and regional progress with the United States. The President has welcomed Brazil's leadership in these organizations in executive policy documents. But his rhetoric has not been matched by specific actions.

Appointing an ambassador to UNASUR, like the United States already does for the European Union (EU) and the Organization of American States (OAS), is one measure that would immediately demonstrate practical U.S. support for regional "economic and security mechanisms," as stated in the NSS. There are benefits for the United States in doing so. Latin American multilateral institutions like UNASUR provide an alternative to Hugo Chavez's version of Bolivarianism within the region, a definite concern of the United States. Instead of criticizing the policies of the Venezuelan regime directly, Brazil has decided to use its own example of establishing generally good relations throughout the world to encourage Hugo Chavez to act more rationally than he would if confronted directly about his radical tendencies. This approach has apparently worked.[40] By participating as an active observer in regional organizations, and by establishing formal diplomatic relations with UNASUR, the United States would do much to extinguish any lingering doubts about the "Colossus of the North."[41]

Brazil's regional activism enables the United States to focus its diminishing foreign aid budget on the unstable parts of the developing world. These proposed diplomatic initiatives are good faith measures crafted to lay the groundwork for greater friendship. They should allay Brazilian concerns regarding sovereignty and reciprocity. Additionally, more positive U.S. – Brazil relations will facilitate future bilateral cooperation on economic and defense measures regionally and throughout the world.

Military Recommendations

Strengthened military relations naturally flow from improved diplomatic ones. As regional leaders, the United States and Brazil can focus their combined security efforts and resources against common threats to the two nations—and to the entire Western Hemisphere. Intelligence sharing during the upcoming World Cup and Olympic games, coordinated counterterrorism measures in the Tri-Border Area, and disrupting narco-trafficking between South America and Africa are among the more pressing security cooperation initiatives that can bring greater security to both countries and to the hemisphere. Close security and defense cooperation in the future, absent the historic shadow of U.S. imperialism, will help in re-establishing the "Unwritten Alliance" dynamic between the United States and Brazil that flourished in the first half of the 20th Century.

When Brazil hosts the World Cup and Olympics in a couple of years, it is in the U.S. national interest to assist Brazil's efforts in countering terrorism, curbing drug trafficking, and reducing international crime. This United States provided similar support to South Africa during the World Cup in 2010 – assisting the prevention of devastating terrorist attacks on that world stage. Averting another "Munich" is certainly in the interest of the United States and indeed of all world sporting events. For the 2010 World Cup, South African security services benefited from security grants and extensive training: "Specifically, Anti-Terrorism Assistance has provided Underwater Explosive, Critical Incident, and Special Events Management, Chemical, Biological, Radiological, Nuclear, and related equipment training."[42] Both the 2006 World Cup in Germany and the following one in South Africa transpired successfully with low-key U.S. security assistance. There were no terrorist attacks, despite ongoing large-scale operations against terrorists in Iraq and Afghanistan at the time. When President Obama visited Brazil in 2011, one of the agreements resulting from the trip was a Memorandum of Understanding (MOU) between the U.S. and Brazil concerning world sporting events cooperation. Security was one of the MOU's six focus areas of cooperation. This MOU is foundational for the U.S. Department of State and Defense to provide any future support desired by the Brazilian government.[43]

One of the great strengths of the United States resides in its intelligence databases, whose holdings and effectiveness have grown substantially since 9/11. For the 2014 World Cup and the 2016 Summer Olympics in Brazil, an intelligence sharing mechanism would help deter terrorism threats. Successful physical or virtual sharing could continue afterwards to address other regional security threats, such as drug trafficking or organized crime. Of course, extending temporary intelligence sharing after the world sporting events may be problematic due to Brazilian memory from its authoritarian past, when the military regime collected intelligence to deter internal dissent.[44] U.S. officials have the next four years to convince the Brazilian government of its benign intentions. With less than two years before the opening kick of 2014 World Cup, beta testing of this provisional intelligence sharing arrangement should begin immediately to track terrorist threats likely to originate in the "Tri-Border Area" of South America.

<u>Exposed Southern Flank</u>

The United States has long worried about the "Tri-Border Area" (The TBA is the name given to the area surrounding the border shared between Brazil, Argentina, and Paraguay). In these border towns, laws are minimally enforced, money is laundered, and weapons, drugs, and people are trafficked. Organized crime and Islamic extremism have thrived there due to a lack of effective law enforcement from the three border nations.[45] Concerns increased after 9/11 that Al-Qaeda could transit potentially porous borders, perhaps through Mexico, to attack U.S. interests in North America.[46] Today, as the specter of war with Iran rises because of its purported pursuit of nuclear weapons, the concern has moved from devastating attacks from Al-Qaeda to devastating attacks from Hezbollah and its patron Iran. As recently as October 2011, Iran was accused of authorizing and financing an assassination attempt against the Saudi Arabian Ambassador to the United States and of contemplating further attacks in Argentina.[47] Successful terrorist attacks against Argentina were carried out in 1992 and 1994 by a Hezbollah militant organization supported by Iran. Terrorists exploited the TBA during each operation.[48] The most telling evidence of potential terrorist attacks out of the TBA surfaced during a Hezbollah militiaman's interview by the Spanish television station

Telemundo. During the interview, the Hezbollah militant stated emphatically that if the United States attacked Iran, then Hezbollah would conduct retaliatory attacks inside the United States.[49] One counterterrorism expert, Edward Luttwak, described Hezbollah's most important base outside Lebanon as the TBA from which they have already supported terrorist attacks: "The northern region of Argentina, the eastern region of Paraguay and even Brazil are large terrains, and they have an organized training and recruitment camp for terrorists."[50]

The historical evidence of terrorist activity emanating from the TBA is chilling. If the current crisis with Iran is not resolved by the time of the 2014 World Cup and the 2016 Olympics, then the Brazilian government will need substantial help in preventing potential terrorist attacks to disrupt games that will attract a global audience. Even now, Hezbollah terrorists may be inclined to strike at Israeli or American targets in the Western Hemisphere in retaliation for a recent UNSC resolution that placed additional sanctions on Iran. Hezbollah attacked its targets in Argentina for lesser reasons in 1992 and 1994.[51] This is why intelligence sharing with Brazil must start now. The last time the United States held a 3+1 Group Meeting (Brazil, Paraguay, Argentina, and the United States) on TBA security was in 2004.[52] This Group should re-convene at the earliest opportunity to assess the current terrorist threat within the TBA and to determine the probabilities of Hezbollah becoming operational if Iran is attacked.[53] Nevertheless, collaborative intelligence initiatives must extend to the World Cup and Olympic timeframes if Iran continues to violate UNSC resolutions concerning its nuclear program. It is in both countries national interests to prevent attacks against their homeland. Certainly, Brazil does not want its territory utilized as a springboard for attacks within the region. Full cooperation in this security arena will assist in preventing the unthinkable until the Iran crisis over-dual use nuclear material is resolved.

Narco-Terrorist Connection

Cooperation in breaking the Brazil—West Africa narcotics connection is another area where national interests converge. In 2009, Brazil became the primary embarkation point for South American cocaine headed for West Africa. In West Africa, "there is evidence by the U.S. Drug Enforcement Agency (DEA) that Latin American traffickers are collaborating with Al-Qaeda in the Islamic Maghreb (AQIM) and Hezbollah to smuggle cocaine to Europe."[54] The Executive Director of the U.N. Office of Drugs and Crime (UNODC) also confirmed that terrorists from Africa used money from drug trafficking to resource operations, purchase equipment, and provide salaries for their ranks.[55] It is common knowledge that the United States conducts counterterrorist operations against AQIM, and seeks to stop any funding derived from the transshipment of cocaine from Latin America. Although Brazil itself does not produce significant amounts of cocaine, it does have 10,500 miles of mostly unsecured coastline. In addition, three of the world's top producers of cocaine border Brazil: Columbia, Peru, and Bolivia. Brazil has invested more heavily in enforcing its borders since the economic boom, but the United States could assist by continuing the same intelligence sharing mechanism that has been proposed for the World Cup and Olympics. Additionally, Brazil's unmanned aerial surveillance (UAS) program is currently in its infancy; it could benefit from the experience and systems of the mature U.S. programs.[56] Building on the predicted intelligence successes of the World Cup and Olympics, this cooperation could perhaps expand to neighboring countries. Eventually, it could evolve into a hemispheric security network serving the national interests of all participating nations.

<u>Brazil's Initiative for Cooperation</u>

The last area of convergence and cooperation is not an American one, but a Brazilian one. Brasília is as interested as the United States in a stronger relationship. The former Brazil Foreign Minister who is now the Defense Minister, Celso Amorin, recognized that there was enormous potential for structured cooperation between Brazil and the United States in areas of the world like Africa where there is great need for development and stability.[57] Minister Amorin has cited the trilateral cooperation agreement among Brazil, Guinea-Bissau, and the United States as an example of productive cooperation. This was a first of its kind agreement for the United States and Brazil in Africa.[58]

These trilateral agreements make strategic sense because bilateral agreements between the United States and relatively poor countries usually elicit criticism that the world's only superpower is engaging in exploitive neo-colonialism. Having itself been a Portuguese colony, Brazil is viewed as a moderating influence on perceived expansive U.S. foreign policy. Brazil is also considered a friendly observer to the Non-Aligned Movement (NAM) of 120 countries that are distrustful of superpower diplomacy.[59] Plainly spoken, if Brazil is part of an U.S. agreement with an impoverished country, that country feels more comfortable making an agreement with the United States because Brazil, a guarantor of U.S. intentions, is part of it. Brazil welcomes this role because it enhances its position as a regional and world leader, establishes a singularly special diplomatic relationship with the United States, and fulfills two of

Brazil's foreign policy action areas.[60] And its role as a third party broker does not end with Africa or other poor regions. Brazil sees itself as a viable broker for peace as evidenced with its last-ditch diplomatic effort with Iran that attempted to resolve the uranium processing crisis.[61]

Minister Amorin shared his idea to expand trilateral frameworks to Secretary Clinton during President's Rousseff's inauguration. Although she seemed open to it at the time, there is no evidence of further action.[62] An opportunity presented, one hopes that this was not an opportunity missed with Brazil. It aligns impeccably with President Obama's pursuit of more partnerships and greater burden-sharing.

Conclusion

With the war in Iraq over and the war in Afghanistan winding down, the United States has the opportunity to re-assess its global strategic interests. In doing so, U.S. leaders must carefully scrutinize Brazil as a long-term strategic partner. A new era of security cooperation with Brazil supports the interests of both nations and strengthens the Western Hemisphere. Collaboration on World Cup and Olympic security is vitally important to the whole world. Many hemispheric homelands are at risk if war breaks out with Iran for whatever reason. Also, drug lords moving narcotics from South America to Europe through Africa represent new relationships of convenience that provide funds for AQIM or other terrorists that further converge U.S.—Brazilian interests.[63] As Brazil grows, so will its security concerns.[64] Brazil has become a responsible international player that is seeking greater diplomatic and security cooperation with the United States. Brazil is willing to help secure the hemispheric and global commons to ensure freedom, stability, and prosperity.[65] However, the United States, acknowledging its domineering past in this region, must give a little, to gain a lot. Only then can the

"Unwritten Alliance" be restored.

Endnotes

[1] Joseph S. Nye, Jr., "The Future of American Power: Dominance and Decline in Perspective," *Foreign Affairs 89*, no.6 2-12 (November, December 2010):2-12.

[2] Nominal GDP from "IMF Data Mapper," September 2011, linked from *The International Monetary Fund Home Page*, http://www.imf.org/external/datamapper/index.php (accessed November 10, 2011).

[3] James K. Rose, "BRIC in the Backyard: Brazil's Economic Rise and What it Means for the United States," *Issue Paper: Center for Strategic Leadership, U.S. Army War College*, Vol. 14-11-14 (July 2011) CSL-2.

[4] Roberto Setubal, "The Opportunities and Challenges for President Dilma Rouseff," *Americas Quarterly*, no. 2 (Spring 2011): 63-64. Between 2010 and 2020, Brazil's oil production is projected to grow 109.5%, with crude volumes rising steadily from 2.16mn b/d in 2010 to an estimated 4.53mn. Business Monitor International, "Brazil Oil and Gas Report Q1 2011," November 2010, http://www.researchandmarkets.com/research/799681/brazil_oil_and_gas (accessed January 20, 2012).

[5] Leslie H. Gelb, "Hillary Hits the Mark," *The Daily Beast,* October 14, 2011, http://www.thedailybeast.com/articles/2011/10/14/hillary-clinton-speech-to-economic-club-of-new-york-a-brilliant-moment.html (accessed 13 November, 2011).

[6] Hillary Rodham Clinton, "Economic Statecraft," October 14, 2011, linked from *The United States Department of State Home Page*, http://www.state.gov/secretary/rm/2011/10/175552.htm (accessed November 14, 2011).

[7] Rose, "BRIC in the Backyard," CSL-3. MERCOSUR is also pursuing free trade agreements with both Mexico and Canada.

[8] *The Economic Times,* Trade between India, Brazil and South Africa set to grow to $25 bn by 2015, October 19, 2011, http://articles.economictimes.indiatimes.com/2011-10-19/news/30297859_1_trade-ministers-trade-data-southern-african-customs-union (accessed November 17, 2012).

[9] E. Bradford Burns, *The Unwritten Alliance: Rio-Branco and Brazilian American Relations* (New York: Columbia University Press, 1966), 172. Interestingly, in 1905 the Secretary of State even refused a request for U.S. intervention in Paraguay and Uruguay claiming this was Brazil's

responsibility. E. Bradford Burns, *The Unwritten Alliance: Rio-Branco and Brazilian American Relations* (New York: Columbia University Press, 1966), 172.

[10] *Elihu Root, Speeches Incident to the Visit of Secretary Root to South America: July 4 to September 30, 1906* (Washington, D.C: Government Printing Office, 1906), 61. A term derived from Secretary of State Elihu Root's speech given to the Federal Senate of Brazil in Rio de Janeiro on August 6, 1906. This term was used to describe the strong diplomatic relationship between Brazil and the U.S. from 1906 to 1942 when a formal alliance was signed between the two countries: "Let us know each other better; let us aid each other in the great work of advancing civilization; let the United States of North America and the United States of Brazil join hands, not in formal written treaties of alliance, but in the universal sympathy and confidence and esteem of their peoples – join hands to help humanity forward along the paths we have been so happy as to tread."

[11] Brazil exercises this role through its renowned diplomatic corps, the Itamarty. The foreign ministry, known as *Itamaraty* after the Neo-classical palace where it was first housed, has the reputation as one of the most effective diplomatic corps in the world. According to Brazilian writer Clarice Lispector, "Itamarty's reputation for strict meritocracy attracted many of Brazil's best minds. And its diplomats' talent in ensuring the nations security without resort to war gave them near mythical aura of competence in a country that generally had little confidence in its governors."

[12] Bodman and Wofensohn, *Global Brazil*, 46.

[13] Meyer, *Brazil—U.S. Relations, 11.*

[14] Einaudi, "Brazil and the United States: The Need for Strategic Engagement," 7.

[15] One example of this is Brazil's accommodation with the Landless Workers Movement. "Brazil's Landless Workers Movement, Movimento dos Trabalhadores Rurais Sem Terra (MST) in Portuguese, is a mass social movement, formed by rural workers and by all those who want to fight for land reform and against injustice and social inequality in rural areas." Friends of the MST, http://www.mstbrazil.org/whatismst (accessed February 02, 2012).

[16] Celso Amorim, "Reflections on Brazil's Global Rise," *Americas Quarterly*, no. 2 (Spring 2011): 50-55.

[17] Even war-torn Colombia has nearly defeated the Revolutionary Armed Forces of Colombia (FARC) insurgency.

[18] Walter Russell Mead, "US To China and Brazil: Take Up the White Man's Burden," *The American Interest*, November 9, 2011, http://blogs.the-american-interest.com/wrm/2011/11/09/us-to-china-and-brazil-take-up-the-white-mans-burden/ (accessed 14 November 2011).

[19] Constitution of the Federative Rebublic of Brazil, 3rd Edition (Brasília: Documentation and Information Center, 2010), Title I, Article 4.

[20] Ibid, Preamble. "We, the representatives of the Brazilian People, convened in the National Constituent Assembly to institute a Democratic State, for the purpose of ensuring the

exercise of social and individual rights, liberty, security, well-being, development, equality and justice as supreme values of a fraternal, pluralist and unprejudiced society, founded on social harmony and committed, in the internal and international orders, to the peaceful settlement of disputes, promulgate, under the protection of God, this Constitution of the Federative Republic of Brazil."

[21] Maria Luiza Ribeiro Viotti, "Security Council Explanation of Vote - Resolution on Iran," *Permanent Mission of Brazil to the United Nations*, June 09, 2010, http://www.un.int/brazil/speech/10d-mlrv-csnu-explanation-vote-iran-0906.html (accessed 14 November 2011).

[22] Former Director General of the International Atomic Energy Agency (IAEA), Dr. Mohammad El Baradei supported Brazil's and Turkey's request for more time to work through their accord with Iran before imposing sanctions. Despite losing the sanctions vote, Brazil did state emphatically they supported the U.N. goal of ensuring Iran's nuclear program was for peaceful purposes only. Ibid.

[23] United Nations, SC/10200/, "Security Council Approves 'No-Fly Zone' Over Libya, Authorizing 'All Necessary Measures' to Protect Civilians, By Vote of 10 in Favour with 5 Abstentions," February 16, 2012, http://www.un.org/News/Press/docs/2011/sc10200.doc.htm, (accessed February 4, 2012).

[24] Frederic Wehrey, "Bringing Libya Under Control," *New York Times*, February 24, 2012, ttp://www.nytimes.com/2012/02/25/opinion/bringing-libya-under-control.html (accessed February 27, 2012); "Libya fighting: Four die in Gaddafi loyalists clash." Fredric Wehrey, a senior policy analyst at the RAND Corporation, described Libya as teetering "dangerously on the brink." "A year after the Libyan revolt began, a weak transitional government confronts armed militias and mounting public frustration. Defiant young men with heavy weapons control Libya's airports, harbors and oil installations. Tribes and smugglers rule desert areas south of the capital. Clashes among various militias for turf and political power rage." *BBC News Africa*, January 23, 2012, http://www.bbc.co.uk/news/world-africa-16690010 (accessed January 24, 2012).

[25] United Nations, GA/11207/Rev.1*, "General Assembly Adopts Resolution Strongly Condemning 'widespread and systematic' Human Rights Violations by the Syrian authorities," February 16, 2012, http://www.un.org/News/Press/docs/2012/ga11207.doc.htm, (accessed February 4, 2012).

[26] Brazil's position is maturing. Along with other countries involved in the Libyan vote. Brazil, felt protecting civilians in Libya did not authorize the violent overthrow of the Libyan government. This time they are more cautious as is most of the rest of the world including the Arab League.

[27] "IMF Data Mapper," September 2011, linked from *The International Monetary Fund Home Page*, http://www.imf.org/external/datamapper/index.php (accessed November 10, 2011).

[28] Purchasing Power Parity (PPP) determines relative size of the economy based on adjusted parity of currencies for all goods and services in a year. It is most useful in discussing measures of GDP and individual relative incomes and costs, but usually not optimal in discussing entire nations' GDPs as it relates to international trade. For example, PPP GDP will appropriately explain whether an American, a Chinese, or a Brazilian can afford food and housing right in their own domestic market since it accounts for trade inside the country as well.

Nominal GDP explains how much value an economy produces as agreed upon by the current world market (e.g. U.S. produces X, China produces Y, and Brazil produces Z). Nominal GDP is the preferred measurement when discussing international trade relative to other countries.

[29] Anonymous, "Leaders: Brazil takes off," *The Economist*, November 14, 2009): 15.

[30] "India - Kashmir (1947 - first combat deaths);" Ploughshares, March 31, 2011, http://www.ploughshares.ca/content/india-kashmir-1947-first-combat-deaths (accessed November 14, 2011). Project Ploughshares reported 752 fatalities from this conflict in 2009 and 2010; and total casualties since 1988 are reported to be 43,000.

[31] Samuel W. Bodman and James D. Wolfensohn, *Global Brazil and U.S. – Brazil Relations* (New York: Council on Foreign Relations, 2011), 47.

[32] Barack Obama, "Remarks by the President to the People of Brazil in Rio de Janeiro, Brazil," March 20, 2011, linked from *The White House Home Page*, http://www.whitehouse.gov/the-press-office/2011/03/20/remarks-president-people-brazil-rio-de-janeiro-brazil (accessed November 15, 2011). "Let us stand together—not as senior or junior partners, but as equal partners, joined in a spirit of mutual interest and mutual respect, committed to the progress that I know we can make together."

[33] Bodman and Wofensohn, *Global Brazil*, 48.

[34] Barack Obama, *National Security Strategy* (Washington, DC: The White House, May 2010), 3.

[35] Luigi R. Einaudi, "Brazil and the United States: The Need for Strategic Engagement," *Strategic Forum*, March, 2011): 1.

[36] "IMF Data Mapper," September 2011, linked from *The International Monetary Fund Home Page*, http://www.imf.org/external/datamapper/index.php (accessed November 10, 2011).

[37] "What is the South American Defense Council?" *Just the Facts*, June 09, 2010, http://justf.org/blog/2010/06/09/what-south-american-defense-council (accessed 14 November 2011). Additionally, during the first Extraordinary Meeting of the Ministers of Foreign Affairs and Defence of UNASUR in November 2009, the South American ministers invited the United States "to a dialogue in relation to the strategic matters of defence, peace, security and development." Strangely, this invitation was not acted upon despite the rhetoric of the NMS that encouraged SADC efforts to "help build interdependence and further integrate partner states into a South American security architecture that will improve regional stability." The United States lost another opportunity to dialogue at the third meeting of the SADC on November 10, 2011, when no American representatives attended. Undoubtedly, the U.S. Government should immediately respond to these requests for dialogue. A lack of response to these initiatives adds to the perception of inattention the United States gives to South America and the rest of Latin America. At the very least, the United States should request to attend the SADC meetings with observer status. M.G. Mullen, *The National Military Strategy of the United States 2011: Redefining America's Military Leadership, 11.*

[38] Peter J. Meyer, *Brazil—U.S. Relations* (Washington D.C: U.S. Library of Congress, Congressional Research Service, July 29, 2011), 13.

[39] Barack Obama, *National Security Strategy,* 44.

[40] Bodman and Wofensohn, *Global Brazil,* 55.

[41] Thomas P. Anderson, *Politics in Central America: Guatemala, El Salvador, Honduras, and Nicaragua* (Westport, CT: Praeger Publishers, 1988), 225. A popular phrase coined by Nicaragua's most famous poet, Rubén Darío. It generally described the United States in bugaboo form. Starting with Monroe Doctrine in 1823, the United States to its advantage, heavily influenced Latin America's political and commercial scene until the end of the Cold War. Unfortunately, this included collusion in overthrowing governments it found unfriendly to U.S interests.

[42] Jana Winter, "U.S. Helps South Africa Beef Up Security for World Cup After Al Qaeda Threats," *Fox News,* April 09, 2010, http://www.foxnews.com/world/2010/04/09/helps-south-africa-beef-security-world-cup-al-qaeda-threats/, (accessed January 24, 2010).

[43] U.S. Department of State, "Memorandum of Understanding between the U.S. and Brazil on Cooperation to Support the Organization of Major Global Sporting Events," March 19, 2011, http://www.state.gov/documents/organization/158857.pdf, (accessed February 26, 2012).

[44] Reuters, "World Briefing, The Americas; Brazil: Suspensions for Domestic Spying," *New York Times,* September 2, 2008, http://query.nytimes.com/gst/fullpage.html?res=9805E6DB1E3FF931A3575AC0A96E9C8B63, (accessed 27 February 2012). Brazilian intelligence agencies are slowly moving from collecting against internal dissent to focusing on external threats. This sensitivity to domestic spying readily became apparent when in 2008 Lula suspended the entire Brazilian Intelligence Agency (Agência Brasileira de Inteligência; ABIN) leadership on reports that the organization was collecting intelligence on the Supreme Court Chief and members of Congress.

[45] Glenn Curtis, *Terrorist and Organized Crime Groups in the Tri-Border Area (TBA) of South America,* (Washington, D.C: Library of Congress, July 2003 revised December 2010). The Tri-Border Area focuses on three hubs of activity: Foz de Iguazu (Brazil), Puerto Iguazu (Argentina), and Ciudad del Este (Paraguay). In this vacuum, radical Islamic organizations like Hezbollah and Hamas thrive.

[46] Mark S. Steinitz, "Middle East Terrorist Activity in Latin America," *Policy Papers on the Americas,* Volume XIV, Study 7, July 2003). "The 9/11 attacks show that Al Qaeda operatives can go undetected for significant periods of time and slip beneath the counterterrorist radar. In addition, the group has, at the least, probed Latin America. Reports that bin Laden himself visited Brazil in the 1990s are unconfirmed, but senior planner Khalid Sheikh Mohammed traveled there in 1995, a fact that came to light following his capture in Pakistan in March 2003. U.S. forces in Afghanistan searching Al Qaeda facilities found travel advertisements for the so-called tri-border area of Paraguay, Argentina, and Brazil, where several Middle Eastern terrorist groups have operated for over a decade."

[47] Richard Esposito and Brain Ross, "Iran 'Directed' Washington, D.C., Terror Plot, U.S. Says," *ABC News,* October 11, 2011, http://abcnews.go.com/Blotter/us-iran-tied-terror-plot-washington-dc-disrupted/story?id=14711933#, (accessed January 24, 2012).

[48] William R. Long, "Islamic Jihad Says It Bombed Embassy; Toll 21," *Los Angeles Times*, March 19, 1992, http://articles.latimes.com/1992-03-19/news/mn-5905_1_islamic-jihad, (accessed January 24, 2012); "Breakthrough made in '94 Argentina bombing," *Associated Press,* November 9, 2005, http://www.msnbc.msn.com/id/9983810/ns/world_news-terrorism/t/breakthrough-made-argentina-bombing/ (accessed 24 January 2011); Ronen Bergman, *The Secret War with Iran: The 30-Year Clandestine Struggle Against the World's Most Dangerous Terrorist Power* (New York: Simon and Schuster, 2008) 172; Robert Baer, CIA Case Officer (Retired), interviewed by Neil Docherty, PBS Frontline, March 22, 2002, http://www.pbs.org/wgbh/pages/frontline/shows/tehran/interviews/baer.html, (accessed January 24, 2012). In the interview, Mr. Baer stated that "Hezbollah's divided into many parties....Then there's the Islamic Resistance, which is an army, which is a guerrilla force, fighting for control of its own country. And then, under the Hezbollah umbrella was the Islamic Jihad, which I call their special security, which was controlled by Iran, which carried out terrorism against the West."

[49] Pablo Gato and Robert Windrem, "Hezbollah builds a Western base, *MSNBC*, May 9, 2007, http://www.msnbc.msn.com/id/17874369/ns/world_news-americas/t/hezbollah-builds-western-base/#.TzgJ1pikdCo (accessed January 24, 2012).

[50] Ibid; According to the Center for Strategic and International Studies, "Edward Luttwak is a CSIS senior associate and has served as a consultant to the Office of the Secretary of Defense, the National Security Council, the U.S. Department of State, the U.S. Army, Navy, and Air Force, and a number of allied governments as well as international corporations and financial institutions;" http://csis.org/expert/edward-n-luttwak; (accessed 24 January 2012).

[51] Ibid.

[52] U.S. Department of State, "Communique of the 3 + 1 Group on Tri-Border Area Security," December 6, 2004, http://www.state.gov/p/wha/rls/70992.htm, (accessed January 24, 2012). It states: "On December 6 and 7, 2004, the delegations of Argentina, Brazil, Paraguay and the United States of America met in the city of Washington D.C. in the framework of the 3 + 1 Group on Tri-Border Area Security to discuss and analyze preventive actions against terrorism and other transnational crimes. The discussions focused on joint activities taken over the previous year by the parties, such as training, international counterterrorism obligations, and best practices for improving law enforcement cooperation, including combating money laundering and terrorist financing."

[53] Although moderate gains have been made against organized crime within the TBA, the principal concern is regarding Hezbollah's illegal fund-raising that remains largely unaddressed because Hezbollah is not listed as a terrorist organization in the TBA countries. U.S. Department of State, *Country Reports On Terrorism 2010*, (Washington D.C: U.S. Department of State, Office of the Coordinator for Counterterrorism, August, 2011), 132, 163.

[54] Nancy Brune, "The Brazil—Africa Narco Nexus," *Americas Quarterly*," no. 3 (Fall 2011): 59-62.

[55] Antonio Maria Costa, "Africa Under Attack," *United Nations Office on Drugs and Crime*, December 8, 2009, http://www.unodc.org/unodc/en/about-unodc/speeches/2009-08-12-africa-under-attack.html, (accessed February 12, 2012).

[56] Other imagery capabilities might provide the identity of remote airfields and parked aircraft used for the cocaine smuggling. If sovereignty issues arise because U.S. Intelligence, Surveillance, and Reconnaissance (ISR) assets are operating within Brazil, the United States could then operate from international waters to provide stand-off intelligence support of suspected inbound drug aircraft coming from Africa.

[57] Amorim, "Reflections on Brazil's Global Rise," 55.

[58] It was soon followed by another one in Senegal regarding ethanol production.

[59] BBC News, "Profile: Non-Aligned Movement," August 07, 2009, http://news.bbc.co.uk/2/hi/2798187.stm, (accessed February 04, 2012).

[60] Meyer, *Brazil—U.S. Relations, 11.*

[61] Even Syria asked Brazil to mediate a peace agreement with Israel. Diehl and Fuji, "Brazil Challenges International Order by Backing Iran Fuel Swap."

[62] These trilateral agreement frameworks were accomplished while Minister Amorin was Brazil's Foreign Minister and Condoleeza Rice was U.S. Secretary of State. Amorim, "Reflections on Brazil's Global Rise," 55.

[63] What worries security officials most is that the illicit routes to South America actually run in both directions. It is feasible that terrorists could use recently emptied drug-hauling planes in Africa to fly back into South America. Brazil could help prevent this importation of terrorists if it expanded its role in multi-national military operations that provide sea and air control. Scott Baldauf, "Air Al Qaeda: Are Latin America's drug cartels giving Al Qaeda a lift?" *Christian Science Monitor*, January 15, 2010, http://www.csmonitor.com/World/2010/0115/Air-Al-Qaeda-Are-Latin-America-s-drug-cartels-giving-Al-Qaeda-a-lift, (accessed February 24, 2012).

[64] Brazil's increased participation in multi-lateral peacekeeping operations is another area of mutual interest and convergence with the United States. Since one of Brazil's diplomatic areas of action is "supporting multilateralism by pushing for the democratization of global governance." Brazil can do more. The primary means to accomplish this goal is through Brazil's historic and consistent support to the United Nations. As one of the founding members of the United Nations, Brazil has participated in 33 peacekeeping operations, and is the 10th largest contributor to the U.N. budget. Since its establishment in 2004, Brazil has provided command and control to the United Nations Stabilization Mission in Haiti (MINUSTAH), and also leads the United Nations Interim Force in Lebanon (UNIFIL) Maritime Task Force off the coast of Lebanon. Seeking additional bona fides as an emerged world power and a responsible international player, Brazil still needs to do more. It is in U.S. interests for Brazil to expand their U.N. peacekeeping or multi-national roles for two reasons. First, it helps fulfills President Obama's desire to "create opportunities in burden sharing" through building partnerships. And, it helps U.S. Department of Defense priorities with capable allies and partners like Brazil to "assure access to and the use of the global commons." Brazil can do this by expanding its participation in U.N. or other multi-national military missions like the Combined Maritime Forces, which is responsible for counter piracy efforts off the coast of Africa, or maritime security operations in the Red Sea, Arabian Sea, Gulf of Aden, and the Persian Gulf. For Brazil, any increased contribution to maintain international order throughout the world positively communicates its intentions to fulfill its global responsibilities commensurate to its economic

rise. Something China nor India have not done yet. It also provides further tangible evidence of responsible behavior and international leadership as Brazil pursues its primary goal of obtaining a permanent seat on the UNSC; Meyer, Brazil—U.S. Relations, 11; Brazil in the Security Council; February 2011, http://www.un.int/brazil/book/conselhoSecuranca_index.html; (accessed January 24, 2012); United Nations Secretariat, Assessment of Member States' contributions to the United Nations regular budget for 2012, 27 December 2011, http://www.un.org/ga/search/view_doc.asp?symbol=ST/ADM/SER.B/853, (accessed January 24, 2012) ; UNIFIL Maritime Task Force, http://unifil.unmissions.org/Default.aspx?tabid=1523, (accessed January 24, 2012); Leon Panetta, "Sustaining U.S. Global Leadership: Priorities for 21st Century Defense," January 2012; http://www.defense.gov/news/Defense_Strategic_Guidance.pdf (accessed February 4, 2012) President Obama's Introduction Letter, 3; Combined Maritime Forces, http://www.cusnc.navy.mil/cmf/cmf_command.html, (accessed February 12, 2012)

[65] Leon Panetta, "Sustaining U.S. Global Leadership: Priorities for 21st Century Defense," January 2012; http://www.defense.gov/news/Defense_Strategic_Guidance.pdf (accessed February 4, 2012), 3

www.ingramcontent.com/pod-product-compliance
Lightning Source LLC
Chambersburg PA
CBHW080807290526
45790CB00008B/3605